GREAT BRITISH THINGS TO Bake AND DO

SAMANTHA MEREDITH
SALLY MORGAN

D0239120

SCHOLASTIC

Scholastic Children's Books,
Euston House, 24 Eversholt Street,
London NW1 1DB, UK

A division of Scholastic Ltd
London ~ New York ~ Toronto ~ Sydney ~ Auckland
Mexico City ~ New Delhi ~ Hong Kong

Editor: Corinne Lucas

Published in the UK by Scholastic Ltd, 2014

Illustrated by Samantha Meredith
Text by Sally Morgan
© Scholastic Children's Books, 2014

ISBN 978 1407 14045 2

Printed in Malaysia.

2 4 6 8 10 9 7 5 3 1

HOT CROSSWORD

Can you solve the clues to find the missing ingredients?
All of them can be found in this book.

ACROSS
1. Single, double, whipped or clotted (5 letters)
3. Self-raising or plain? (5 letters)
4. Puff-ect for pies or Eccles cakes (6 letters)
7. Peel to get to the core (5 letters)
8. The American name for them is 'cookies' (8 letters)
9. Get cracking yolks (4 letters)

DOWN
1. Bar or chips? Plain or milk? Melt over water (9 letters)
2. Gives bread a rise (5 letters)
5. Plain ice-cream flavour (7 letters)
6. Grated skin of an orange or lemon (4 letters)
8. Churned milk (6 letters)
10. The sweet stuff – caster or icing? (5 letters)

3

MAKE A BAKER'S APRON

Transform an old pillowcase into a super-stylish apron to keep your threads flour free.

You will need

- Clean pillowcase
- ruler
- felt-tip pen
- 3 pieces of 70 cm-long ribbon
- scissors
- needle
- thread.

1. Turn the pillowcase inside out and lay it on a table, with the open end nearest to you.

2. Use a ruler to measure 12 cm in from each corner of the closed end, and mark with a felt-tip pen.

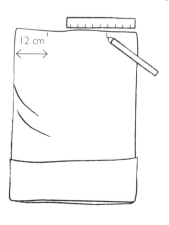

3. From each of your first marks, measure and draw a vertical line 20 cm long. Connect the bottom of each of these lines to the edge of your pillowcase, to make two rectangles.

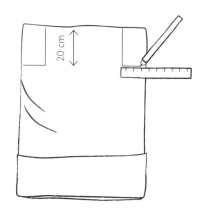

4. Draw another two lines 1.5 cm inside the lines already drawn to create two right angles, as shown by the dotted line.

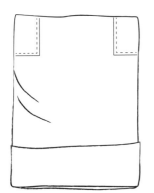

5. Cut out both of the smaller rectangles, leaving the first lines you drew showing on the pillowcase.

6. Using a needle and thread, sew down the longest line, then turn the corner and sew along the horizontal line. Secure your sewing with a few knots and snip away any excess thread. Repeat on the other corner. This will make sure your apron has neat edges. Now turn the pillowcase the right way round so it's no longer inside out.

7. Take one piece of ribbon and stitch each end to the top corners of the back of your apron. This will form a loop that will go over your head.

8. Take the other two pieces of ribbon and stitch one to each of the centre corners of your pillowcase, as shown. These will tie around your waist.

Great British tip
Need your apron in a hurry? Instead of sewing your pinny together, try using fabric glue.

SHREWSBURY BISCUITS

These fruity biscuits come from Shrewsbury, in the West Midlands. They are mentioned in cookbooks as early as the 1650s.

Ingredients
- 125 g butter, room temperature, plus extra for greasing
- 150 g caster sugar
- 2 egg yolks
- 225 g plain flour, plus extra for dusting
- 75 g currants
- 1 tbsp lemon zest, grated.

Equipment
- Grater, for the zest
- 2 large baking trays
- kitchen paper
- large bowl
- wooden spoon
- rolling pin
- 6 cm circular fluted cutter.

1. Ask an adult to preheat the oven to 180°C/gas mark 4.

2. Use kitchen paper to grease two large baking trays with butter.

Warning! *Make sure you ask an adult to help you whenever you'd like to use the oven.*

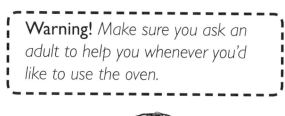

3. Cream the butter and sugar together in a large bowl with a wooden spoon until the mixture is light and fluffy.

6

4. Add the egg yolks and stir until they are all mixed in.

5. Stir in the flour, lemon zest and currants until you have a crumbly dough that you can squash together with your hands.

6. Sprinkle flour onto your work surface and rolling pin and put the dough on top of it. Roll out the dough until it is 0.5 cm thick.

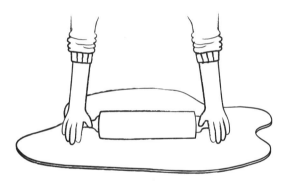

7. Use your circular fluted cutter (one with crinkly edges) to cut out as many biscuits as you can from the dough.

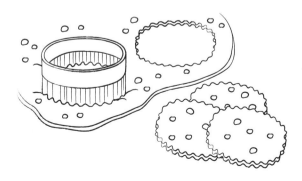

8. Press together any leftover dough, then roll it out again and cut out more biscuits until you've used up all of the dough so there's none wasted.

9. Place the biscuits onto the baking trays and ask an adult to put them in the oven for 15 minutes, or until they are beginning to turn a pale golden colour.

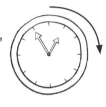

10. Leave to cool and enjoy.

Great British tip
If you store your biscuits in an air-tight container, like an old sweet tin or a Tupperware, they will last a lot longer.

CORNISH FAIRINGS

These spicy little biscuits used to be sold at fairs all over Cornwall. They are delicious with a glass of cold milk.

Ingredients
- 225 g plain flour
- 2 tsp baking powder
- 1 ½ tsp baking soda
- 1 tsp mixed spice
- 1 tsp cinnamon
- 2 tsp ground ginger
- 100 g butter, cut into cubes
- 1 whole lemon zest, grated
- 100 g caster sugar
- 4 ½ tbsp golden syrup.

Equipment
- Table knife, to cube the butter
- grater, for the zest
- large baking tray
- greaseproof paper
- large bowl
- wooden spoon
- tablespoon.

1. Ask an adult to preheat the oven to 180°C/gas mark 4.

2. Take a large baking tray and line it with greaseproof paper.

Warning! *Make sure you ask an adult to help you whenever you'd like to use the oven.*

3. Pour the flour, baking powder, baking soda and spices into a large bowl and mix together well.

4. Add the butter and use your fingertips to rub it into the flour until there are no large lumps of butter left. Your bowl should look like it is full of crumbs. Add the zest and the sugar and stir well.

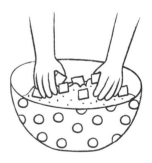

5. Add the syrup and mix together with your hands until you have a soft dough.

8

6. Use a tablespoon to take lumps of dough and shape them into walnut-sized balls between your palms.

7. Place the dough balls on your baking tray, 5 cm apart.

8. Ask an adult to put the baking tray into the oven for 10 minutes, until they have spread out into golden, crackle-topped biscuits. Leave to cool and enjoy.

HOT CROSS BUNS

Nothing says springtime in Great Britain more than hot cross buns!

Ingredients

- 200 ml milk
- 50 g butter, plus extra for greasing
- 500 g strong white bread flour
- 3 tsp mixed spice
- 50 g caster sugar
- 7 g sachet of fast-action yeast
- pinch of salt
- 2 eggs, beaten
- 200 g currants
- 75 g plain flour, plus extra for dusting
- 4 tbsp water
- 1 tbsp golden syrup.

Equipment

- 3 bowls – 2 small, 1 large
- fork, to beat the egg
- large baking tray
- kitchen paper
- saucepan
- wooden spoon
- 2 tea towels
- sandwich bag
- pastry brush.

> **Warning!** *Make sure you ask an adult to help you whenever you'd like to use the hob or the oven.*

1. Use kitchen paper to grease a large baking tray with butter.

2. Ask an adult to bring the milk to the boil in a saucepan, then remove it from the heat. Add the butter and stir until it melts. Leave to cool for 10 minutes.

3. Mix the strong white bread flour, spice, sugar, yeast and salt together in a large bowl. Pour in the warm milk and butter mixture. Add the beaten eggs and stir until you have a sticky dough.

4. Sprinkle the spare flour onto your work surface and put the dough on top of it. Knead the dough by squashing and squeezing it

between your hands and against the work surface for 10 minutes, until it is smooth and squashy.

5. Put the dough back into your bowl and cover with a tea towel. Leave in a warm place for 1 hour.

6. Take the tea towel off the bowl. The dough should have doubled in size.

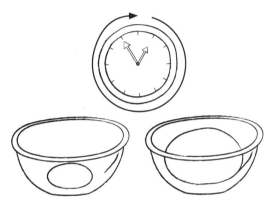

7. Tip in your currants and knead the dough again until the fruit is all mixed in.

8. Split your dough into 12 equal pieces and shape them into balls by rolling them between your palms. Place the balls of dough onto your baking tray, 5 cm apart. Cover with a clean tea towel and leave in a warm place for 1 hour.

9. Ask an adult to preheat the oven to 220°C/gas mark 7.

10. For the icing, mix the plain flour and the water in a small bowl and spoon into a sandwich bag. Carefully snip a small corner off the bag and gently squeeze two lines of flour paste onto the top of each bun to make a cross.

11. Ask an adult to pop your buns into the oven for 15 minutes, or until golden brown.

12. Brush with golden syrup and then leave to cool for 10 minutes. Split in half, spread with butter and enjoy.

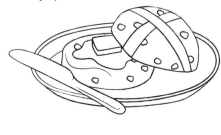

HOT CROSS MAZE

Can you find your way to the other side of this delicious tray of buns? Careful, they're hot!

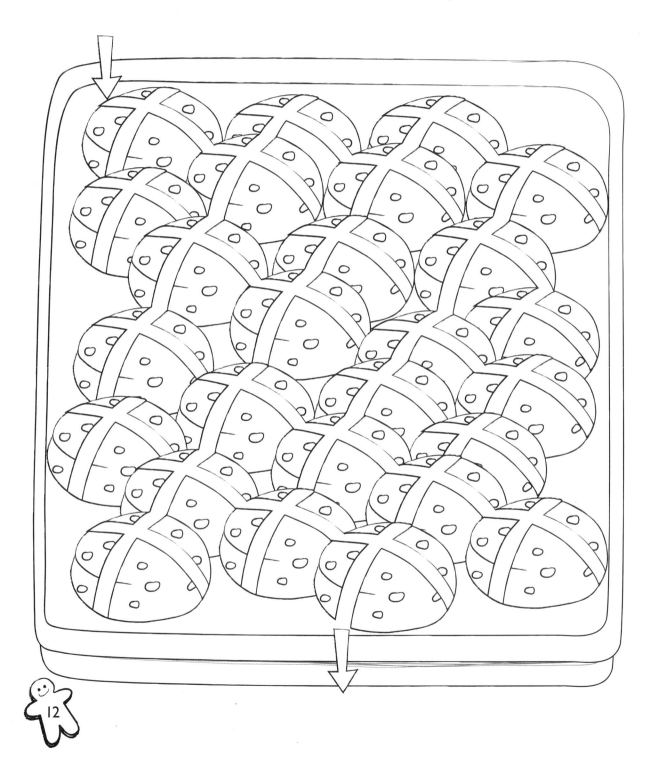

FLAPJACKS

Chewy and oaty – perfect for walks in the countryside.

Ingredients

- 300 g butter, cut into cubes, plus extra for greasing
- 5 tbsp golden syrup
- 100 g soft brown sugar
- pinch of salt
- 500 g rolled oats.

Equipment

- Table knife, to cube the butter
- rectangular cake tin
- kitchen paper
- large saucepan
- wooden spoon.

1. Ask an adult to preheat the oven to 180°C/gas mark 4.

2. Use kitchen paper to grease the inside of a cake tin with butter.

3. Ask an adult to slowly melt the remaining butter (300 g) in a large saucepan.

Warning! *Make sure you ask an adult to help you whenever you'd like to use the hob or the oven.*

4. Remove the saucepan from the heat. Add the syrup, sugar and salt and stir until all of the sugar has dissolved.

5. Add the oats and stir until they are coated with the sugary butter.

6. Spoon the mixture into your tin, pressing it into the corners and smoothing over the surface.

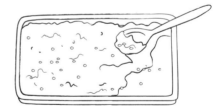

7. Ask an adult to put the tin into the oven for 25 minutes, or until the flapjack is golden.

8. Cut into rectangles using a table knife. Enjoy on a hike in the Great British outdoors.

 # TOTTENHAM CAKE

Squares of Tottenham cake used to be sold for a penny each! They are utterly delicious no matter which football team you support.

Ingredients

- 225 g butter, room temperature, plus extra for greasing
- 225 g caster sugar
- 4 eggs, beaten
- 280 g self-raising flour
- 2 ½ tsp baking powder
- 2 tsp lemon zest, grated
- 4 tbsp milk
- 300 g icing sugar
- 5–6 tbsp water
- 1 drop pink food colouring.

Equipment

- 3 bowls – 2 small, 1 large
- fork, to beat the eggs
- grater, for the zest
- 35 x 25 cm rectangular cake tin
- kitchen paper
- greaseproof paper
- scissors
- 2 spoons – 1 wooden, 1 metal
- wire rack
- palette knife
- table knife.

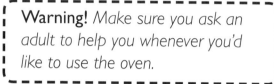

Warning! *Make sure you ask an adult to help you whenever you'd like to use the oven.*

1. Ask an adult to preheat your oven to 180°C/gas mark 4.

2. Use kitchen paper to grease the inside of a cake tin with butter. Line it with greaseproof paper.

3. Cream together the butter and sugar in a large bowl by mixing them with a wooden spoon until the mixture is light and fluffy.

4. Add the beaten eggs and beat them into the mixture.

5. Add the flour and baking powder. Fold them into the mixture by going all the way around the edge of the bowl once and then 'folding' the mixture on top of itself into the middle of the bowl. Repeat until all of the flour is mixed in.

6. Finally, add the lemon zest and milk and stir well.

7. Spoon the mix into your tin. Smooth it out with a metal spoon.

8. Ask an adult to put the tin into the oven for 35 minutes, or until golden. Remove from the oven and leave on a wire rack to cool.

9. For the icing, put your icing sugar into a small bowl and add a little water at a time, until you have a smooth runny paste. Add the food colouring and stir until you have an even pink colour.

10. Once the cake is cool, turn it the right way up and pour the icing over your cake. Spread it evenly over the top and sides using a palette knife. Leave to set.

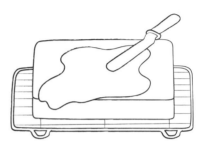

11. Cut your cake into squares using a table knife and enjoy while watching the football.

15

WHAT A MESS

Oh no! Amir's kitchen has got into a real state.
Can you help him find everything he needs to make his Eton mess?

10 × 🍓 8 × 🧄 2 × 🥄 2 × 🥣 1 × 🥄 2 × 🧋 6 × 🍨

16

ETON MESS

This is one mess your parents will be happy
you made in the kitchen this summer.

Ingredients
- 400 g strawberries
- 2 tsp caster sugar
- 500 ml whipping cream
- 8 meringue nests.

Equipment
- Table knife
- colander
- 2 large bowls
- whisk
- metal spoon.

1. Wash your strawberries in
cold water. Cut off the stalks
and cut the strawberries
into quarters using
a table knife. Put
them in a bowl
with the sugar.

2. In another bowl, whisk the
cream until it can hold
its shape on a
spoon.

Great British tip
Whisking cream can take some
time so you may want to ask an
adult's help, or use an electric whisk.

3. Crumble the meringue nests
into the cream. Don't worry if
the pieces are uneven, it all adds
to the mess!

4. Add your strawberries and
sugar and mix everything
together with a metal spoon.
Take care not to mix too hard so
you don't break up the meringue
more than you have to.

5. Serve in a
large pretty
bowl or in
individual
glasses.

ECCLES CAKES

Eccles cakes come from a town called Eccles in north-west England but their flaky yumminess is enjoyed all over Great Britain.

Ingredients
- 75 g butter, plus extra for greasing
- 150 g brown sugar
- 200 g dried mixed fruit
- 1 tsp cinnamon
- ½ tsp nutmeg
- 2 tbsp orange juice
- 500 g ready-made puff pastry
- 2 tbsp milk
- 1 tbsp granulated sugar
- a little flour, for dusting.

Equipment
- Large baking tray
- kitchen paper
- saucepan
- large bowl
- wooden spoon
- rolling pin
- 7 cm circular cutter
- teaspoon
- pastry brush
- table knife.

1. Ask an adult to preheat the oven to 200°C/gas mark 6.

Warning! *Make sure you ask an adult to help you whenever you'd like to use the oven.*

2. Use kitchen paper to grease a large baking tray with butter.

3. Ask an adult to slowly melt the butter in a saucepan. Remove from the heat.

4. Put the sugar, fruit, cinnamon, nutmeg and orange juice into a bowl and carefully add the melted butter. Mix everything together with a wooden spoon.

5. Sprinkle flour onto your work surface and rolling pin, and lay your pastry on top. Roll out the pastry until it's roughly 3 mm thick.

6. Using a 7 cm circular cutter, cut out as many circles from the pastry as you can.

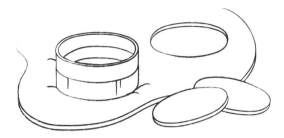

7. Press any leftover pastry together, roll it out again and cut out more circles until you have an even number, so there is no wasted pastry. You might need to add more flour to the rolling pin and the work surface if your pastry is too sticky.

8. Move half your circles onto the baking tray, and place a heaped teaspoonful of fruit mix into the centre of each one. Then, using a pastry brush, brush around the edges of the pastry with milk.

9. Place the rest of the circles on top of the fruit and press around the edges with your fingertips to seal them.

10. Make three slits in the top with a table knife and then brush each cake with a little milk.

11. Sprinkle the top of each cake with sugar.

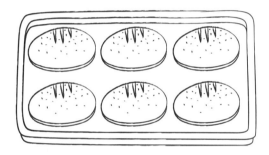

12. Ask an adult to put your baking tray in the oven for around 15 minutes, when the cakes should be crisp and golden.

13. Leave to cool for at least 15 minutes, then tuck in!

WELSH CAKES

These are a delicious tea-time treat, traditionally called 'pice ar y maen' in Welsh.

Ingredients

- 225 g plain flour, plus extra for dusting
- 85 g caster sugar
- 1 tsp mixed spice
- 1 tsp baking powder
- ¼ tsp salt
- 105 g butter, cut into cubes
- 50 g currants
- 1 egg, beaten
- a little milk.

Equipment

- Table knife, to cube the butter
- 2 bowls – 1 small, 1 large
- fork, to beat the egg
- rolling pin
- 7 cm circular cutter
- frying pan
- fish slice
- kitchen paper.

1. Put the flour, sugar, spice, baking powder, salt and 100 g of your butter into a large bowl.

Warning! *Make sure you ask an adult to help you whenever you'd like to use the hob.*

2. Use your fingertips to rub the butter into the dry ingredients. Keep rubbing until all the big lumps have gone and your bowl looks like it is full of crumbs.

3. Add the currants and stir in the beaten egg until you get a stiff dough that you can squash together with your hands. If your mix looks too crumbly, add a little milk. If it's a bit sticky, add some more flour.

4. Sprinkle some flour onto your work surface and rolling pin and roll out your dough until it is 1.5 cm thick. Add a splash more milk if your dough starts to dry out too much.

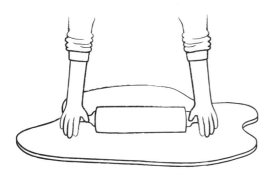

6. Ask an adult to melt the rest of your butter (5 g) in a frying pan over a low heat.

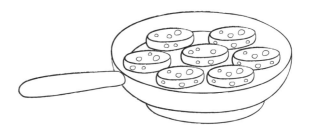

7. Ask an adult to add your cakes to the pan and fry for 3–4 minutes on each side. Carefully scoop them out with a fish slice and leave them to cool on kitchen paper.

5. Use a 7 cm circular cutter to cut circles out of your dough. Squash together any leftover dough and roll it out again. Cut as many circles as you can so there's no wasted dough.

8. Serve your cakes with butter and lots of yummy jam!

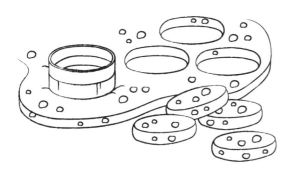

FABULOUS FAIRY CAKES

Fairy cakes are just like their American friends – cupcakes – but smaller and even easier to make.

Ingredients

- 265 g butter, room temperature
- 115 g caster sugar
- 2 eggs, beaten
- 1 tbsp milk
- 1 tsp vanilla essence
- 115 g self-raising flour
- ½ tsp baking powder
- 300 g icing sugar
- 2 tbsp milk.

Equipment

- 3 bowls – 1 small, 2 large
- fork, to beat the eggs
- wooden spoon
- whisk
- 2 x 12-hole bun tins
- paper cases
- teaspoon
- wire rack
- table knife.

Warning! *Make sure you ask an adult to help you whenever you'd like to use the oven.*

1. Ask an adult to preheat the oven to 180°C/gas mark 4.

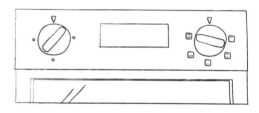

2. Put 115 g of your butter and all of the caster sugar into a large bowl. Mix with a wooden spoon until the mixture is light and fluffy.

3. Add the beaten eggs, milk and vanilla essence. Whisk together.

4. Add the flour and baking powder and whisk together until you have a smooth mixture.

22

5. Fill two 12-hole bun tins with paper cupcake cases. Use a teaspoon to half fill each of the cases with your mixture.

6. Ask an adult to put your fairy cakes into the oven for 10 minutes and leave to cool on a wire rack.

7. For the buttercream icing, put the rest of the butter (150 g) into a large bowl and beat with a wooden spoon until it is light, fluffy and a pale yellow colour.

8. Add 150 g of the icing sugar and stir until is all mixed in. Then add the rest of the icing sugar and mix together again.

9. Stir in the milk a little at a time until you have a smooth mixture.

10. Use a table knife to carefully cut a circle off the top of each of your cakes, creating a small hole. Put the spare pieces of cake to one side and fill the holes with a dollop of icing.

11. Using a table knife, cut each the spare piece of cake in half and push the two halves into the icing, so they look like wings.

Great British tip:
Make your fairy cakes extra special by adding food colouring to your icing with sprinkles on top.

FAIRY FINISHES

Decorate the icing and cases of these fairy cakes
so they look yummy enough to eat!

FLAG-TASTIC CAKE PLATTER

Serve your delicious cakes on a Union Jack cake platter.

You will need

- Dinner plate
- large cardboard box
- felt-tip pen
- scissors
- blue tissue paper
- 2 pieces of 30 x 4 cm white ribbon
- 2 pieces of 30 x 2 cm red ribbon
- sticky tape.

1. Place a dinner plate on one side of the cardboard box, draw around it with a felt-tip pen and carefully cut it out.

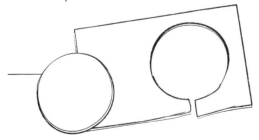

2. Cover one side of your circle with tissue paper and carefully secure it on the underside of the circle with sticky tape. Don't pull too tight or the paper might tear.

3. Take your white ribbon and arrange it on your circle in a diagonal cross. Lay the red ribbon over the top of the white ribbon, in the centre.

4. Tuck the ends of the ribbon under the cardboard circle, pull tight and secure to the underside with sticky tape.

5. Next, lay the white ribbon over the top in a cross shape, placing the red ribbon on top of the white ribbon as before. Secure again with sticky tape.

6. Pile high with delicious baked goods.

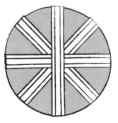

SEASIDE ROCK BISCUITS

Create minty biscuits with leftover sticks of rock.

Ingredients

- Broken sticks of rock
- 100 g butter, room temperature
- 150 g soft brown sugar
- 100 g granulated sugar
- 1 egg, beaten
- 190 g plain flour
- ½ teaspoon baking powder
- 100 g dark chocolate chips.

Equipment

- 3 bowls – 1 small, 2 large
- fork, to beat the egg
- 2 large baking trays
- sandwich bag
- rolling pin
- wooden spoon
- tablespoon
- wire rack.

Warning! *Make sure you ask an adult to help you whenever you'd like to use the oven.*

1. Ask an adult to preheat the oven to 180°C/gas mark 4.

2. Line two large baking trays with greaseproof paper.

3. Put the sticks of rock into a sandwich bag, seal, and crush with a rolling pin (being careful of your fingers!).

4. Place the butter and sugars in a large bowl and mix with a wooden spoon until the mixture is light and fluffy. Stir in the beaten eggs until it is all mixed in.

5. In another bowl, mix together the flour and baking powder.

6. Add the flour mix to the wet ingredients in the first bowl and stir until it is all mixed together.

26

7. Add the crushed rock and the chocolate chips and mix together gently until they are all combined.

8. Use a tablespoon to place dollops of mixture, the size of ping-pong balls, onto the paper-lined baking trays, 5 cm apart.

9. Ask an adult to put the trays into the oven for 15 minutes, then leave to cool on a wire rack.

How many sticks of rock can you find hidden in this seaside scene?

 # VICTORIA SPONGE

When you taste your jam-filled creation,
you won't believe how easy it is to make.

Ingredients
- 200 g caster sugar
- 200 g butter, room temperature, plus extra for greasing
- 200 g self-raising flour
- 4 eggs, beaten
- . tsp baking powder
- 1 tsp vanilla extract
- 5 tbsp strawberry jam
- 2 tbsp icing sugar.

Equipment
- 2 bowls – 1 small, 1 large
- fork, to beat the eggs
- 2 x 20 cm round cake tins
- greaseproof paper
- pencil
- scissors
- wooden spoon
- sieve
- wire rack.

1. Ask an adult to preheat your oven to 190°C/gas mark 5.

Warning! *Make sure you ask an adult to help you whenever you'd like to use the oven.*

2. Use kitchen paper to grease your two cake tins with butter.

3. Fold a piece of greaseproof paper in half and place one of the cake tins on top. Draw around the tin with a pencil and cut out your circle. You will be left with two circles. Pop one onto the base of each tin.

4. Cream together your butter and sugar by mixing them with a wooden spoon in a large bowl, until the mixture is light and fluffy.

5. Beat the eggs into the mixture.

6. Next, sieve in the flour and fold it into the mixture by going all the way around the edge of

the bowl once and then 'folding' the mixture on top of itself into the middle of the bowl. Repeat until all of the flour is mixed in.

7. Spoon half of the mixture into each tin and spread so it covers the base of the tin evenly.

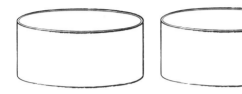

8. Ask an adult to put your tins into the oven for 20 minutes until they are a golden yellow colour.

9. Remove your cakes from the tins and place them on a wire rack until cool.

10. Spread the top of one of your cakes with jam and place the other cake on top.

11. Sprinkle the top with icing sugar and enjoy!

Lucky number 13
Bakers used to get into trouble if they sold their customers light loaves, so they would avoid accidentally cheating people by giving them 13 loaves for every dozen (or 12) that they ordered. That is why a baker's dozen is 13 and not 12.

Victoria what?!
It wasn't just this yummy cake Queen Victoria put her name to. In her lifetime she had plums, peas, flowers, cities and even waterfalls named after her.

The sweet stuff
Ever wondered where sugar comes from? Most of the sugar in Britain comes from sugar beet – big lumpy root vegetables that look like giant parsnips. That doesn't mean it counts as a vegetable though!

GINGERBREAD PEOPLE

It is said that the first gingerbread people were made for Elizabeth I, who asked her cooks to shape gingerbread to look like her favourite guests.

Ingredients

- 350 g plain flour, plus extra for dusting
- 6 tsp ground ginger
- 1 tsp bicarbonate of soda
- 110 g butter, cut into cubes, plus extra for greasing
- 175 g soft brown sugar
- 5 tbsp golden syrup
- 1 egg, beaten
- a few currants.

Equipment

- Table knife, to cube the butter
- 2 bowls – 1 small, 1 large
- fork, to beat the egg
- 2 large baking trays
- kitchen paper
- rolling pin
- gingerbread person cutter.

1. Ask an adult to preheat the oven to 180°C/gas mark 4.

> **Warning!** *Make sure you ask an adult to help you whenever you'd like to use the oven.*

2. Use kitchen paper to grease two large baking trays with butter.

3. Put the flour, ginger, bicarbonate of soda and butter in a large bowl. Rub the butter into the dry ingredients with your fingertips until the mixture looks like breadcrumbs.

4. Pour in the sugar, syrup and egg and squash it all together until you have a firm dough.

5. Dust your work surface and rolling pin with the spare flour. Roll out the dough until it is 5 mm thick.

6. Use a gingerbread person cutter to cut out as many people as you can from your dough.

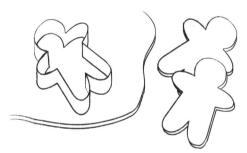

7. Press together any leftover dough, roll it out again and cut out as many biscuits as you can, so there's no wasted dough.

8. Place your gingerbread people on your greased baking tray. Press two currants into the head of each of your people, for eyes.

9. Ask an adult to put your baking trays into the oven for 10–12 minutes until the biscuits are light brown and then leave to cool.

Great British tip
Use icing and sweets to give your people some super-sweet outfits. Try out some designs on these gingerbread people with pens and pencils.

WHILE-IT-BAKES WORDSEARCH

Distract yourself from those delicious smells coming from the oven by trying to find all of your equipment in the wordsearch.

Baking tray
Bowl
Cake tin
Cutter
Fork

Loaf tin
Oven
Saucepan
Scales
Scissors

Spatula
Tablespoon
Teaspoon
Wire rack
Wooden spoon

B	D	G	P	P	S	U	R	F	N	I	H	I	T	Z
N	O	O	P	S	N	E	D	O	O	W	P	C	E	E
Y	D	W	Z	Y	T	I	O	V	W	T	A	K	A	H
U	A	S	L	T	X	P	E	I	C	E	L	E	S	T
Q	L	R	U	S	S	N	R	G	D	V	U	R	P	S
Z	J	C	T	E	C	E	I	Y	N	N	T	P	O	E
K	Z	W	L	G	R	I	J	T	P	G	A	A	O	L
Z	T	B	V	A	N	Q	S	T	F	A	P	T	N	A
K	A	P	C	A	K	I	Z	S	W	A	S	Q	F	C
T	K	K	N	O	A	X	K	M	O	J	O	R	O	S
N	I	T	E	K	A	C	S	A	T	R	K	L	R	N
S	A	U	C	E	P	A	N	D	B	H	S	V	K	P

CHOCOLATE FUDGE

There are only four ingredients between you and lip-lickingly good fudge.

Ingredients
- 500 g chocolate, in pieces
- 60 g butter, cut into cubes
- 1 tsp vanilla essence
- 1 × 397 g can sweetened condensed milk

Equipment
- Table knife, to cube the butter
- 20 × 20 cm square cake tin
- tin foil
- scissors
- saucepan
- table knife.

1. Cover the inside of a 20 × 20 cm cake tin with foil.

2. Add the chocolate, butter and vanilla essence into a saucepan and pour in the condensed milk.

Warning! *Make sure you ask an adult to help you whenever you'd like to use the hob.*

3. Ask an adult to put the pan over a low heat until all of the chocolate is melted. Stir well.

4. Pour the mixture into the cake tin and leave to cool. When cool, place in the fridge and leave to set for 3 hours.

5. Remove from the fridge and cut into pieces with a table knife.

Great British tip
Take a pretty gift box, line it with tissue paper and pop in your fudge to make a sweet gift for a friend.

MYSTERY BAKER

From the clues throughout the book,
can you work out who's baked which cake?

Queen Victoria

Welsh baker

Footballer

School boy

Fairy princess

Eton mess

Victoria sponge

Tottenham cake

Fairy cake

Bara brith

35

 # BARA BRITH

This traditional Welsh recipe actually has tea inside the cake!
Tea and cake in one mouthful, delicious.

Ingredients
- 225 g mixed dried fruit
- 400 ml strong, hot tea, no milk
- knob of butter
- 175 g self-raising flour
- 175 g wholemeal flour
- 1 tsp baking powder
- 1 ½ tsp mixed spice
- 60 g soft brown sugar
- 1 egg, beaten.

Equipment
- 3 bowls – 1 small, 2 large
- fork, to beat the egg
- teapot
- large loaf tin
- kitchen paper
- wooden spoon
- wire rack.

1. Put the dried fruit in a bowl and pour over the hot tea. Stir together and leave the fruit to soak overnight.

Warning! *Make sure you ask an adult to help you whenever you'd like to use the oven.*

2. Ask an adult to preheat the oven to 160°C/gas mark 3.

3. Use kitchen paper to grease the inside of a loaf tin with butter.

4. Tip both flours, the baking powder, spice and sugar into a large bowl and stir together.

5. Pour in the beaten egg and the fruit, along with any tea still in the bowl. Mix together until the fruit is evenly spread in the mixture.

6. Spoon your mixture into the loaf tin. Squash it into the corners and smooth on the top.

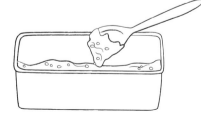

7. Ask an adult to put your cake in the oven for 1 hour and 20 minutes and then leave to cool for 10 minutes.

8. Remove your loaf from the tin and place on a wire rack to cool.

9. Cut up your loaf, spread the slices with butter and enjoy with more tea.

Complete the grid so that there is just one tea cup, flag, daffodil and piece of bara brith in each row, column and group of four squares.

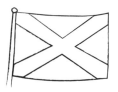 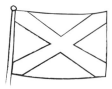

SCOTTISH MACAROONS

Make these and you will never look at a spud in the same way.

Ingredients
- 100 g potatoes
- 2 tbsp butter
- 1 tbsp milk
- 3 drops vanilla essence
- 500 g icing sugar
- 100 g desiccated coconut
- 300 g dark chocolate, in pieces.

Equipment
- Potato peeler
- table knife
- 2 saucepans
- colander
- 20 x 20 cm square cake tin
- large baking tray
- greaseproof paper
- 2 bowls – 1 small, 1 large
- sieve
- wooden spoon
- greaseproof paper
- a large plate.

Warning! *Make sure you ask an adult to help you whenever you'd like to use the hob.*

1. Carefully remove the skin of the potatoes with a peeler. Chop them in half with a table knife.

2. Put the potatoes into a saucepan and cover with water. Ask an adult to bring them to the boil, then simmer for 15–20 minutes until the potatoes are soft all the way through.

3. Drain the potatoes in a colander, then return to the pan

and add the butter and milk, and mash until they are smooth with no lumps. Leave to cool.

4. Line a 20 x 20 cm cake tin and a baking tray with greaseproof paper.

5. Put the mashed potato and vanilla essence into a large bowl. Sieve roughly one third of the icing sugar into the mixture. Stir until all the sugar is mixed in. Add another third and stir again. Add the rest of the icing sugar until you have a sticky paste.

6. Spoon the mix into the cake tin and spread into the corners. Put it into the freezer for 2 hours.

7. Ask an adult to heat the oven to 160°C/gas mark 3.

8. Sprinkle the coconut onto the baking tray. Ask an adult to put it into the oven for 3–4 minutes or until golden and leave to cool.

9. Ask an adult to bring a pan of water to the boil. Remove from the heat. Put the chocolate into a bowl and place the bowl on top of the pan. Leave it to stand for 5 minutes. Stir the chocolate to check it's all melted.

10. Take the potato mix out of the freezer and cut it into small bars using a table knife.

11. Ask an adult to help you dip each bar into the melted chocolate and then roll it in the coconut.

12. Place the bars onto a plate covered in greaseproof paper, and put them in the fridge to set.

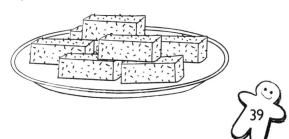

CHOCOLATE CONKERS

What better way to celebrate autumn than with a heap of yummy chocolate conkers?

Ingredients
- 360 g smooth peanut butter
- 1 tsp vanilla essence
- 120 g butter, room temperature
- 400 g icing sugar, sifted
- 300 g dark chocolate, in pieces.

Equipment
- Sieve, for the icing sugar
- large baking tray
- greaseproof paper
- 2 bowls – 1 small, 1 large
- wooden spoon
- tablespoon
- saucepan
- fork.

1. Take a large baking tray and line it with greaseproof paper.

2. Mix the peanut butter, vanilla essence, butter and icing sugar in a bowl with a wooden spoon until it forms a thick dough.

Warning! *Make sure you ask an adult to help you whenever you'd like to use the hob.*

3. Scoop out conker-sized lumps of dough using a tablespoon. Shape the lumps of dough into balls by rolling them between your palms.

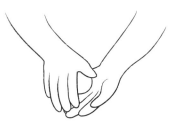

4. Lay each ball onto the baking tray, and put the sheet into the fridge to chill for 1 hour.

5. To melt the chocolate, ask an adult to bring a pan of water to the boil and then remove it from the heat.

40

6. Put your chocolate pieces into a small bowl and place the bowl on top of the pan. Leave it to stand for 5 minutes. Give the chocolate a stir to check that it has completely melted.

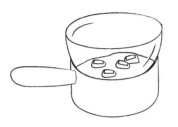

8. Pull your fork out and put the chocolate-covered ball back onto your baking tray, chocolate-side down. Repeat for the rest of your peanut-butter balls. Put them back in the fridge for 20 minutes to set.

9. Pile your conkers up and enjoy with a glass of cold milk.

7. Push a fork into a peanut-butter ball and dip the ball into the chocolate. Leave a small circle of the peanut-butter dough showing.

AUTUMN-LEAF GIFT BOX

Give a chocolate conker to a friend
in this gorgeous autumn-leaf gift box.

You will need
- Colouring pencils
- scissors
- chocolate conker.

1. Colour in the box template on the opposite page and then turn over the page and colour in the other side. This will be the inside of your box.

2. Cut out the coloured box template using a pair of scissors.

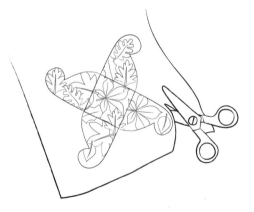

3. Fold the template along each of the dotted lines.

4. Place a chocolate conker in the centre of your box.

5. Take two opposite flaps and connect them together by folding them towards the centre and slotting them together.

6. Repeat step five with the other two opposite flaps, connecting them over the top of the first pair. Beautiful!

Great British tip
Want to give conkers to lots of friends? Simply trace the template rather than cut it out to make as many gift boxes as you like.

42

43

44

APPLE CRUMBLE

This British pudding is easy to make and the perfect way
to round off a traditional Sunday lunch.

Ingredients
- 100 g caster sugar
- 225 g butter, cut into cubes
- 210 g plain flour
- 450 g cooking apples, cut into 1.5 cm chunks
- 75 g soft brown sugar.

Equipment
- Table knife, to cut the butter and apples
- 2 large bowls
- wooden spoon
- large ovenproof dish.

1. Ask an adult to preheat the oven to 190°C/gas mark 5.

2. Put the caster sugar, butter and 200 g of flour into a large bowl. Rub the butter into the mixture, using your fingertips, until you have no big lumps of butter left and the mixture looks like breadcrumbs.

3. Put your chunks of apple into another bowl. Stir together with the brown sugar and 10 g of flour.

4. Tip your apple mix into a large ovenproof dish and cover evenly with your crumble topping from your first bowl.

5. Ask an adult to put the crumble into the oven for 1 hour until golden brown.

6. Leave to cool for 10 minutes before dishing up with lots of custard.

FAT RASCALS

These Yorkshire scones date back to Elizabethan times.

Ingredients
- 300 g self-raising flour, plus extra for dusting
- ½ tsp baking powder
- 130 g butter, cut into cubes
- 100 g caster sugar
- 1 tsp mixed spice
- 150 g mixed dried fruit
- zest of 1 orange, grated
- zest of 1 lemon, grated
- 50 ml double cream
- 2 eggs, beaten
- 50 g glacé cherries, halved
- 25 g flaked almonds.

Equipment
- Table knife, to cube the butter and halve the cherries
- 2 bowls – 1 small, 1 large
- fork, to beat the eggs
- grater, for the zests
- large baking tray
- greaseproof paper
- wooden spoon
- rolling pin
- pastry brush.

Warning! *Make sure you ask an adult to help you whenever you'd like to use the oven.*

1. Ask an adult to preheat the oven to 200°C/gas mark 6.

2. Take a large baking tray and line it with greaseproof paper.

3. Mix the flour and baking powder in a large bowl. Add the butter and use your fingertips to rub in the butter until your bowl looks like it is filled with crumbs.

4. Add the sugar, spice, dried fruit and zests, and stir together.

5. Add the cream and half of the egg mixture, and stir until you have a soft dough.

6. Dust your surface with flour and roll out the dough until it's 2.5 cm thick. Divide the dough into six pieces, shape into rounds and put them on the baking tray.

7. Brush each bun with the remaining egg. Press a cherry and almonds into the top of each bun.

8. Ask an adult to put them into the oven for 15 minutes until golden and then leave to cool.

9. Slice them in half and spread with clotted cream and strawberry jam. Yum!

STICKY TOFFEE PUDDING

This gooey dessert is perfect to warm you up on a cold winter day.

Ingredients

- 175 g dates, chopped
- 1 tsp baking soda
- 300 ml boiling water
- 195 g butter, room temperature, plus extra for greasing
- 170 g caster sugar
- 2 eggs, beaten
- 225 g plain flour
- 1 tsp baking powder
- 1 tsp vanilla essence
- 270 g soft brown sugar
- 300 ml double cream.

Equipment

- Table knife, to chop the dates
- 2 bowls – 1 small, 1 large
- fork, to beat the eggs
- ovenproof dish
- kitchen paper
- wooden spoon
- saucepan
- jug.

Warning! *Make sure you ask an adult to help you whenever you'd like to use the hob or the oven.*

1. Put the dates and baking soda into a bowl. Ask an adult to pour over the boiling water. Soak for 1 hour.

2. Ask an adult to preheat the oven to 200°C/gas mark 6.

3. Use kitchen paper to grease your ovenproof dish with butter.

4. Put 70 g of butter, all of the caster sugar, beaten eggs, flour, baking powder and vanilla essence into a bowl. Mix them together until you have a sloppy mixture. Stir in the dates and any leftover soaking water.

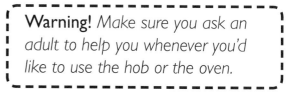

5. Spoon the mixture into the ovenproof dish. Ask an adult to put it into the oven for 40 minutes. Leave it to cool for 10 minutes.

6. For the sauce, put the remaining butter (125 g), brown sugar and double cream into a saucepan and ask an adult to bring it to the boil for 3 minutes.

7. Pour the sauce into a jug and serve with the pudding.

Great British tip
You can also serve your pudding with a dollop of vanilla ice cream for a bit of extra luxury.

Three young bakers have entered their creations into the village show. Can you work out who got first, second and third place?

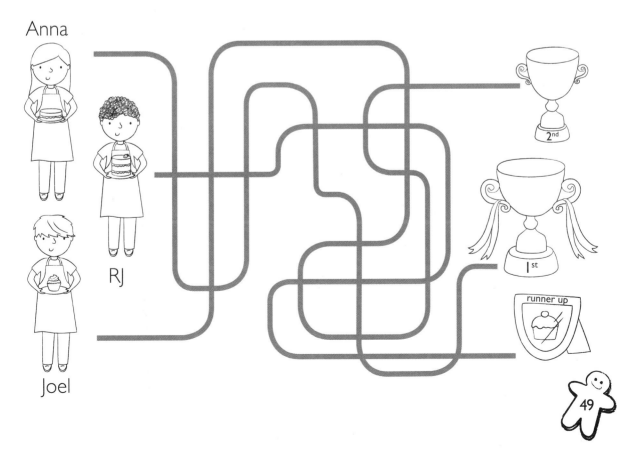

Anna

RJ

Joel

2nd

1st

runner up

49

SALT-DOUGH DECORATIONS

Decorate your room, or even your Christmas tree, with these doll and dino creations that you can keep forever!

You will need

- Paper
- pencil
- scissors
- large bowl
- spoon
- 150 g salt
- 300 g plain flour, plus extra for dusting
- 150 ml water
- rolling pin
- table knife
- garlic press
- paints
- paintbrushes
- PVA glue
- ribbon.

Warning! *Make sure you ask an adult to help you whenever you'd like to use the oven.*

1. Trace over the template of the doll or dinosaur on the next page with paper and a pencil. Cut it out.

2. Ask an adult to preheat your oven to its lowest temperature.

3. Put the salt and flour into a large bowl and mix together. Add a little water at a time, stirring continuously until you have a smooth dough that you can squash with your hands. If your dough feels too sticky, add a sprinkle more flour. If it feels too dry and keeps cracking, add a splash more water.

4. Dust your surface and rolling pin with flour. Roll out your dough until it is 1.5 cm thick. Place your template onto the dough and cut around it with a table knife. Cut as many decorations as you can.

5. Use a pencil to make a hole in the top of each decoration, as shown on the template.

6. Use the leftover dough to add detail to your decorations. Push some dough through a garlic press to make hair for your dolls, or cut out small triangles to make scales for your dinos. Stick your detail on using a little water.

7. Place them on a baking tray and ask an adult to put them in the oven for 3–4 hours, or until firm. Remove and leave to cool.

8. Paint your decorations bright colours. Once dry, apply a coat of PVA glue for a shiny finish.

9. Thread your ribbon through the hole in your decorations and secure with a knot. Hang them up or give as gifts.

51

MINCE PIES

Christmas wouldn't be Christmas without a warm mince pie.
This year, why not try making your own?

Ingredients
- 300 g shortcrust pastry
- 1 × 175 g jar mincemeat
- 1 egg, beaten
- 1 tbsp icing sugar
- a little flour, for dusting.

Equipment
- Small bowl
- fork, to beat the eggs
- rolling pin
- 10 cm circular cutter
- 12-hole bun tin
- teaspoon
- 7 cm circular cutter
- pastry brush.

Warning! *Make sure you ask an adult to help you whenever you'd like to use the oven.*

1. Ask an adult to preheat your oven to 200°C/gas mark 6.

2. Sprinkle flour onto your work surface and rolling pin. Roll out your pastry until it is 3 mm thick.

3. Use a 10 cm circular cutter to cut out 12 pastry circles.

4. Place your pastry circles into a 12-hole bun tin, pressing each one gently into place.

5. Use a teaspoon to place a blob of mincemeat onto each circle.

6. Use a 7 cm circular cutter to cut 12 lids from the rest of your pastry. Place a circle on top of each of your pies. Brush with egg.

7. Ask an adult to put them in the oven for 10–15 minutes.

8. Sprinkle with icing sugar and serve warm. Delicious!

BREAD AND BUTTER PUDDING

This yummy pudding is easy to make and a great way to use up any leftover hot cross buns or teacakes.

Ingredients
- 5 hot cross buns
- 50 g butter
- 50 g raisins
- 1 tin of custard (approx. 400g)
- 150 ml milk
- 2 tbsp light brown sugar.

Warning! *Make sure you ask an adult to help you whenever you'd like to use the oven.*

Equipment
- Table knife
- ovenproof dish
- jug.

1. Ask an adult to preheat the oven to 200°C/gas mark 6.

2. Slice the buns in half and butter each half.

3. Cut the buns into quarters and then arrange neatly in the bottom of an ovenproof dish, butter-side down. Sprinkle your raisins over the top.

4. Pour the custard into a jug, add the milk and stir together.

5. Pour the mixture over the buns, making sure they are completely covered. Sprinkle sugar over the top.

6. Ask an adult to put your pudding into the oven for 35 minutes, until the top is golden brown and crispy.

BAKER'S DOZEN

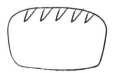

Can you spot a baker's dozen (13) differences between these two scenes?

MICROWAVED STEAMED PUDDING

Traditional steamed puddings can take hours to boil on the stove.
Try this quick recipe for a delicious alternative.

Ingredients
- 100 g butter, room temperature
- 100 g caster sugar
- 1 tsp vanilla essence
- 2 eggs, beaten
- 1 tbsp milk
- 100 g self-raising flour
- 3 tbsp your favourite jam.

Equipment
- 2 bowls – 1 small, 1 large
- fork, to beat the eggs
- jug
- wooden spoon
- microwaveable dish.

1. Mix the butter and sugar in a large bowl until light and fluffy.

2. Put the vanilla, egg and milk in a jug and stir. Pour the liquid a little at a time into the butter and sugar until you have a smooth mixture and then stir in the flour.

> **Warning!** *Make sure you ask an adult to help you whenever you'd like to use the microwave.*

3. Put the jam into the bottom of a microwaveable dish and then pour the mixture over the top.

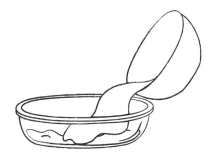

4. Ask an adult to cook in the microwave on high power for 4 minutes. Leave to stand for 2 minutes before serving. It goes best with lots of custard.

Great British tip
Swap the jam for syrup, lemon curd or fruit for different flavours.

56

KITCHEN COOL

Design an ace apron and pair of oven gloves for your dream kitchen.

57

TOP SPOTS

Use your keen detection skills to find out which page each of these images appeared on throughout the book.

A

B

C

D

 # GREAT BRITISH BAKES

This book is filled with brilliant bakes from around Great Britain. Can you draw a line from each bake to the country they were traditionally baked in?

59

CORNISH SAFFRON BUNS

Saffron can be very expensive, but you only need to use a little pinch to make these yummy yellow buns.

Ingredients

- Pinch of saffron
- 1 tbsp hot water
- 600 g white bread flour, plus extra for dusting
- pinch of salt
- 125 g butter, cut into cubes, plus extra for greasing
- 7 g sachet of fast-action yeast
- 80 g caster sugar
- 1 egg, beaten
- 150 ml milk
- 100 ml water
- 175 g currants.

Equipment

- Table knife, to cube the butter
- 3 bowls – 1 small, 2 large
- fork, to beat the egg
- egg cup
- 2 large baking trays
- kitchen paper
- wooden spoon
- cling film
- wire rack.

Warning! *Make sure you ask an adult to help you whenever you'd like to use the hob or oven.*

1. Put the saffron in an egg cup and ask an adult to add the hot water. Leave to stand for 15 minutes.

2. Use kitchen paper to grease two large baking trays with butter.

3. Mix the flour and salt together in a large bowl. Add the cubed butter and use your fingertips to rub it in until your bowl looks like it is filled with crumbs.

4. Add the yeast, sugar and saffron water and mix well.

5. Pour the milk into a saucepan and ask an adult to slowly warm it on the hob.

6. In another large bowl, mix the beaten egg, warm milk and water and then pour it into the flour mixture. Stir together until you have a sticky dough.

7. Sprinkle the spare flour onto your surface and knead the dough for 5 minutes until it is stretchy and smooth.

8. Add the currants and squash them into the dough until they are all mixed in.

9. Break your dough into 12 and shape each piece into a ball.

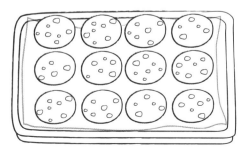

10. Place the balls onto the baking trays, 5 cm apart, and cover loosely with cling film.

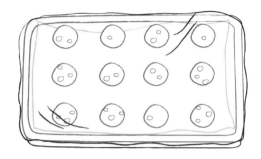

11. Leave in a warm place for 45 minutes. They should have doubled in size.

12. Ask an adult to preheat the oven to 220°C/gas mark 7.

13. Ask an adult to put your buns into the oven for 20 minutes and then leave them to cool on a wire rack.

ALL THE ANSWERS

Hot Crossword page 3
Across: 1. Cream, **3.** Flour, **4.** Pastry,
7. Apple, **8.** Biscuits, **9.** Eggs
Down: 1. Chocolate, **2.** Yeast, **5.** Vanilla,
6. Zest, **8.** Butter, **9.** Sugar

Hot Cross Maze page 12

What a Mess page 16

Hidden Rock page 27

While-it-bakes Wordsearch page 33

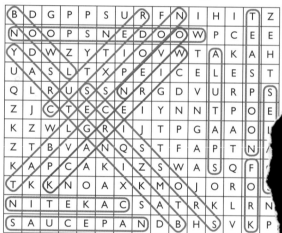

Mystery Baker page 35

Queen Victoria baked the Victoria sponge
The Welsh baker baked the bara brith
The footballer baked the Tottenham cake
The schoolboy baked the Eton mess
The fairy princess baked the fairy cake

Sudoku page 37

Dot-to-dot page 47

It's a chef, of course!

Young Bakers page 49

Anna won first prize
Joel came second
RJ was the runner up

Baker's Dozen pages 54–55

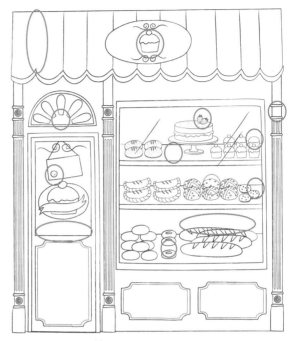

Top spots page 58

page 27

page 41

page 16

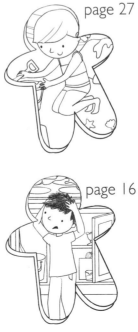

page 15

bara brith

Scotland

Scottish macaroons

Shrewsbury biscuits

Welsh cakes

fat rascals

England

Wales

Eton mess

ALSO AVAILABLE